BUILDING BLOCKS FOR RAISING GODLY CHILDREN

A Foundation of Faith and Values

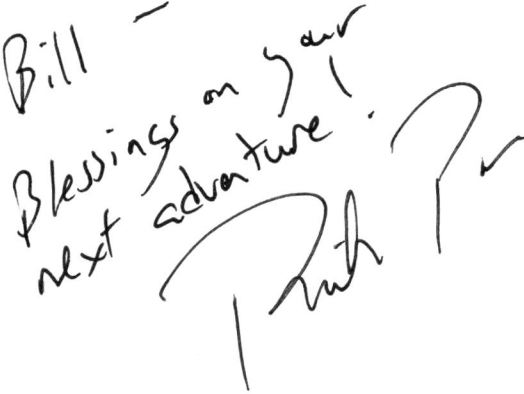

Bill —
Blessings on your
next adventure!
Rick Post

RICK POST

Building Blocks for Raising Godly Children

Rick Post

TABLE OF CONTENTS

Building Blocks for Raising Godly Children

Published by Potential Resources, Little Canada, MN 55109

Cover Design by Justin Post

Hardcover ISBN - 978-0-9996510-2-5	
E-book ISBN	- 978-0-9996510-3-3

Printed in the United States of America

DEDICATION

This book is dedicated to my wife Beth and my children, Justin and Maryn, Kala and Sean, and Colin and Katelyn. Without their support, encouragement and help this book would never have made it to print. They were the ones who showed me through their lives the impact these building blocks could have in building Godly children. They helped me to capture these ideas to share in this book.

It is also for my grandchildren. I pray that they will grow to be Godly men and women just as their parents have become and that they will continue to pass the wisdom to future generations.

> *"The father of godly children has cause for joy. What a pleasure to have children who are wise."*
> *Proverbs 23:24 NLT*

I could not have authored this book without the partnership and support of my wife Beth! She has been there by my side for almost 39 years of marriage. I may have authored the book, but she was the one who helped all the building blocks come together for our kids. I am blessed to have her by my side in the journey of our life together! She is my rock and encourager who always helped me make it through the challenges I have faced over the years.

Thanks to my kids who helped with the design, edits, and content reviews throughout the writing process!

FORWARD

Parenting is one of those topics that there are hundreds of books written about but there are no guaranteed results. Every child is unique and what works for one may not turn out the same way as another. There is no book, method or style of parenting that fits every family or child. So, I thought I would add another book to the options available.

Parenting is like building a brand-new house. You must determine where you want to live, find a piece of property that is available to build on, find a builder, and then decide what kind of house you want to build. That may involve selecting a plan that the builder has already created or collaborating with an architect to draft your plans from scratch. So how does this compare to parenting, you may ask?

Well to begin with, becoming a parent starts with finding someone you love. This involves dating, finding out about them and seeing if you are in love. This compares to the research and finding a plan and builder for your house. Signing a purchase agreement and taking out loan to pay for the house is like your marriage. You say your vows and commit to be together till death do you part. For most, after you are married you decide when the right time to start a family is, how many children you think you want and how far apart each will be. Of course, most experiences never go exactly as planned. This is the building process of the house. You selected the plan and started to build. There is great anticipation as the house nears completion and you are ready to move in. This is like the birth of your child.

Then the process of maintenance of your house is like raising your children and being a parent. There are normal bumps and bruises in life just like there are dents and scratches that happen to your house. Sometimes there are events that cause major damage, and you must rebuild the house, and this happens in your life as well. There may be sicknesses, injuries or relationship failures that cause damage to your family that cause you to have to rebuild the damage that happened.

So, what is the point of this comparison? First, your marriage and becoming a parent is a lifetime commitment. Second, building a house that lasts requires having a good plan that is built on a solid foundation. Third, making that house last requires regular maintenance and investment. This is what this book is all about. It is about the building blocks that go into building Godly children. I will share about establishing a firm foundation and provide some ideas you can use to build a family that stays together and thrives together.

Some background on me. I am the author of this book, but parenting was done together with my wife Beth. I may be writing this, but Beth was truly the glue that made these ideas work. At the time of authoring this book, we have been married for 38 years and have three married children and five grandchildren. What I will be sharing here is a collection of ideas and thoughts that we learned from our years as parents. We certainly made our share of mistakes, and we are constantly learning ideas and ways that we can continue to be better parents and grandparents. These thoughts and ideas do not come from research or academic studies but rather from our own experiences. Read them, see how they fit in your life and apply them with your own variations. **The key to success is not to follow someone else's plans or ideas, but rather to make them your own!**

All of this requires work. You must take time to reflect on what were positive or negative elements of your childhood that you want to incorporate into your marriage and parenting, and be willing to seek professional help, if needed.

The purpose of this book is to give you some practical ideas on how to build a Godly family. It is not written to fix your problems, but rather to give you some ideas of what you can do with your family. This book is written from our perspective and is filled with the lessons we have learned from our mistakes and our successes over the years.

> *"Direct your children onto the right path, and when they are older, they will not leave it."*
> *Proverbs 22:6 NLT*

Using these building blocks does not mean your children will never stray and that you will not have challenges and difficulties. Each person makes their own choices in life, but I believe these will help you provide wisdom to your kids and help them make better choices and hopefully avoid making choices that they regret later. I also understand that there are children with disabilities and parenting may look different for them than what I have shared here.

My hope is that you will read this book with your spouse and with your friends. It could be a useful resource in your small group or Sunday school class. Use the Reflection and Discussion Questions to help you discuss the chapters and how you may want to apply the building blocks to your life. There is also a Guided Prayer section for you to journal your prayers in each chapter.

1 – Your Past Matters

"This explains why a man leaves his father and mother and is joined to his wife, and the two are united into one." Genesis 2 24

When you find your soulmate and decide to get married and one day start a family, you are beginning the process of merging two people with two different backgrounds and family history and are starting a new family history. Moving out of your home and moving in with your new spouse is the easier part. But leaving your past and the way you were raised is not as easy. Add to it that you are marrying someone who has a different past, different parents, and separate ways of doing things makes this much harder than you think or expect.

Each of us has a different story. That story is our history. You cannot change it! The question you need to ask is what do you want to do with this history? Do you want to repeat it, learn from it, or try to heal from it? Your stories are unique, but what you want to do with those stories and how you want to apply them to your families is up to you.

Now, I realize that each person's upbringing is different. You may have had a great childhood with almost perfect parents and experiences that you want to repeat with your family. But my guess is that you have a story filled with some good things and some things that were not so good. I know that there are people who come from family experiences that involved abuse, absentee parents or were raised in single parent homes. You also may have other factors including divorce, step parenting and siblings raised in two different family dynamics.

When you think about all the difficult stories that people bring into the beginning of a family, it is no wonder that so many struggle and have conflicts, often without even knowing why. People think that their past is the past and that they can just start fresh with a new life and have never processed through the things that they have brought with them from their past. Let me be clear – I am not a licensed therapist or a trained counselor. You may have things that you need to deal with professionally. It is never too late to see a counselor to work through the challenges or trauma that you have faced as a child and learn how that has impacted your new family.

Our Background

Both Beth and I came from homes with two parents, and we were raised with traditional Christian values. My father was a pastor of small Baptist churches. I was the youngest of five children and was six years younger than my closest sibling. My father with an authoritative figure who demonstrated control over the family. We attended church for every service whenever the church was open. I was raised in a home where I did not attend movies in the theatre, use Playing Cards or listen to secular music. There was never alcohol or tobacco use in the home. We spent time playing games together before bed many nights of the week. We played ping pong and were competitive with each other. We also played board games like Scrabble and Rook. As a family we would take a vacation together every summer, usually to a cabin in Wisconsin that my parents rented each summer. My parents loved to fish for pan fish and we spent much of our vacation catching and cleaning fish and playing games together.

While most observers would say I was raised in a normal loving home, there were aspects that were not healthy. My father parented with a judgmental, authoritarian style. Our behavior was more important than showing love to each other in our family. Being open and transparent with my feelings or questioning my parents was not encouraged or allowed. I was encouraged to work hard in school, get good grades and ideally attend a Bible school. My parents meant well, as this was how they were raised as children. We were not a hugging, loving family and the words "I love you" were not widely shared. Our language was filled with sarcasm and making fun of each other rather than sharing words of encouragement or love to each other.

As you may guess, these were the things from my past that I brought to our marriage, and resulted in the challenges that we faced as newlyweds. More about that later.

Beth's childhood, which had similar Christian values as mine, also had its differences. Beth was the oldest of three kids. Her parents were missionaries with Wycliffe Bible Translators, and she spent the first 10 years of her life in Papua New Guinea. She returned to the United States at the age of ten and had to learn how to adjust to the American culture. Her family had Swedish roots and their lives had Swedish traditions. Beth was raised in a home that was more expressive of love but was also raised in a performance-based culture, where how you acted and dressed was important. Beth was raised as a "Good Girl" who always did what she was told to do and never caused any troubles for her parents.

When we met in college, our relationship took a while to form. She was dating my roommate and after breaking up with him, she was not interested in me as a boyfriend. Beth's dad worked at the college we attended and one of my jobs there was as a janitor. I cleaned her father's office on a regular basis. I remember seeing Beth's picture on his desk and being interested in her long before I ever met her. After failing on several attempts to get her to date me, she finally agreed to one date, but let me know she was going out "only as friends" and that she had no interest in anything more with me. We went out, had a fun time, but I would never have asked her out again if she had not sent me a note telling me she was interested and would love to go out again.

We dated for a year and got engaged one year later and married a year after that. That time gave us many opportunities to learn about each other and meet each other's family, but there are still things you do not discover until you are married. Dating gives you a chance to see the things a person brings to the marriage, but some things you never discover until after you say, "I DO" and begin your life together.

Once we were married, we had to go from talking about what we wanted our marriage and family to be to living it out and working out the differences we had. Once the honeymoon was over, the challenges of blending a new family together began. Some common things that create these challenges are differences of opinions over things like money and how to spend it, time spent with friends, time spent with parents and family and over sex and different needs and expectations. All are very normal, but how you were raised contributes to the way in which you resolve these issues. If you have never spent time thinking about your past, it may lead to fights or arguments because the root issues have not been addressed yet.

I wish I could tell you we worked out all these problems in the first six months, but it took years to discover the impact of how we were raised and how to work through those challenges and problems. We still have challenges, but we have learned over the years how to better understand who we are, and we are better at expressing our feelings and desires in those situations.

I want to focus on three important things to remember about your past and the impact they have on your future. These are: find a happy balance between your two childhoods; start new traditions; and deal with the issues or trauma you may have from your past. This is a great place to start when building a godly foundation for your children.

FIND A HAPPY BALANCE BETWEEN YOUR TWO CHILDHOODS

As you start your family together, take time to discuss what things you liked about your family and how you were raised, and what things were challenging. As you have children, these experiences will shape decisions on how you raise your children. Not all the things your parents did were bad and not all were good. Do not try to do the opposite of what your parents did as it can have a detrimental effect and as bad of an impact as how you were raised. Focus on finding a balance between the two extremes and make sure you are both in agreement on the approach. And always remember, if a decision is not working the way you wanted it to, it is okay to change the approach. Here are areas were there can be extreme differences of opinion:

Mealtime eating rules

- Eat what you are served vs. eat what you want.
- No dessert if you do not eat your vegetables vs. eat what you want.
- Eat together sitting at the table vs. eat wherever you want.
- No sweets vs. sweets are ok to eat.

Bedtime

- Go to bed when tired vs. have a scheduled bedtime each night.
- Sleep in own bed vs. sleep with parents.

Discipline

- Spanking vs. time outs.
- One warning vs. repeated warnings.
- Consistency of discipline vs. inconsistent discipline.

Let me give you an example about mealtimes and how we chose to manage it when our children were young. I was raised in a home that taught you to eat everything you were served, whether you liked it or not and that you needed to eat everything that was on your plate. Looking back at this, it fits into the authoritarian style of my father and the impact of him being raised during the Great Depression and World War II where money and resources were limited.

If you felt the way you were raised was extreme, find a middle ground instead of trying to do the opposite. Find the balance between what you liked and what you did not like, but always remember, the things you did not like may have been because you wanted to be in control, and you may not have been ready for that. More about that later in the book.

START NEW FAMILY TRADITIONS

Family traditions, especially around holidays, can be a big tension point between families. One spouse may have been raised with one set of traditions and the other had different ones. Our parents often want us to continue with those traditions after we leave home and form our families. It can be hard to decide which family traditions you want to continue with and how to decide which one you will choose to honor. In some cases, you try to keep both family traditions alive, and it makes for stressful and tiring holidays.

Stopping family traditions can be hard. It can result in conflict and hurt feelings. As I mentioned earlier, Beth came from a Swedish family that had strong holiday traditions, especially with the food that was served. For Christmas there was always a Swedish Smorgasbord with all the traditional Swedish foods. I was not Swedish, and these were not foods that were normal for me. They were good, but not my favorites. For years we would gather at Christmas with our extended family for this tradition. It created our own conflicts as I wanted to do other things and Beth as the "Good Girl" did not want to offend so we always had to attend. It was not that the tradition was bad, it was just not mine and the focus was on the tradition more than a time to be together. We always felt the need to dress up and be on our best behavior. Again, not that any of that was bad, but Beth did not want to offend her parents and relatives, so she went along with what she thought was expected of her.

We finally moved on and started our own family traditions. Now as we have adult children and they have their own families, we try to remember not to force them to follow our traditions but rather to form new traditions for themselves. This is not always easy, but extremely healthy.

DEAL WITH THE ISSUES FROM YOUR PAST

This last point can be a hard topic to address but is also one of the most critical issues to deal with. Almost everyone has had trauma in their life. These can range from dealing with the loss of a family member by death or divorce, physical or emotional abuse or some form of sexual abuse. Unfortunately, these traumas were never talked about or dealt with because of the pain and impact that they have had on your life. These traumas often create shame which most people want to bury and never deal with. Failure to deal with the shame of the trauma and understand the impact that it can have on your life can often result in the patterns repeated and cause difficulties in trust, relationships, and intimacy in a marriage.

Both Beth and I had traumas that happened to us in our childhood that were never discussed, except to each other. When events caused these to become exposed it caused us to finally deal with the trauma and understand the impact that it had on our lives and the way we interacted with each other. Seeing a counselor and processing through the impact of childhood trauma has helped us better understand who we are and the ways we acted. Fortunately, we were able to deal with the issues and not pass these behaviors on to our children, but they certainly impacted the mistakes we made and things we had to learn from so we would not repeat them. I thank God that I was able to learn from the impact of how I was raised and made changes before it became a problem that would plague my children as well.

As I mentioned earlier, I was raised in home with an authoritative father who was never wrong and used his words to shame rather than encourage us. I also struggled with this early in our marriage and as we started to have children. I was an authoritarian father who enforced the rules and used sarcasm as my way of communicating. I was not aware of how this behavior was hurting Beth or our children. I had a blind spot, which is often caused by the impact of trauma that is not dealt with. But because Beth was a loving spouse who cared about me and was willing to help me see how this was damaging our marriage and me as a father, she helped me see what I was doing, and I started to make changes because of it. I had to learn how my words impacted her, and my kids and I learned the power of being able to say, "I am sorry."

For Beth, her trauma caused her to become the "Good Girl" who never confronted others and always tried to make everyone happy. Through work with a counselor, she was able to see how this had impacted her and learn to be more open with her feelings and emotions.

I share these examples to point out the importance of not avoiding your past and dealing with it. This book was not written to help you with dealing with trauma. There are great resources available if you need help in this area, but no matter what, deal with it. Deal with your past. Examine your past. Make changes because of your past. Your family's future depends on it!

Reflection Questions:

- Think about how you were raised and write down the positive and negative things you remember.

- How has your childhood impacted your marriage and family?

- What challenges did you face in your marriage regarding how you were raised?

- What does a happy balance look like in your marriage regarding how you were raised? What areas have you had to change to parent from the way you were parented?

- Do you and your spouse have different traditions from your childhood?

- Write out any trauma you have experienced. Have you shared them with your spouse?

- Have you been to a counselor to help your process the impact of your trauma? How has it helped you?

- What is one thing you have taken away from this chapter that you want to discuss with your spouse?

Discussion Questions:

- What does Genesis 2:24 tell us to do?

- Why do you think God wants us to do this?

- How has your childhood impacted your marriage and family?

- What things from your childhood have you tried to repeat in your family?

- What things have you tried to do differently than from how you were raised?

Prayer:

Write a prayer to God committing your parenting to Him and asking Him to help you parent in a Godly way.

_____

_____

_____

_____

_____

_____

_____

_____

_____

_____

_____

_____

_____

_____

_____

_____

_____

_____

_____

_____

_____

_____

_____

2 – BUILDING A FIRM FOUNDATION

"Anyone who listens to my teaching and follows it is wise, like a person who builds a house on solid rock. Though the rain comes in torrents and the floodwaters rise and the winds beat against that house, it will not collapse because it is built on bedrock. But anyone who hears my teaching and does not obey it is foolish, like a person who builds a house on sand. When the rains and floods come and the winds beat against that house, it will collapse with a mighty crash."
Matthew 7:24-27 NLT

After looking at our pasts and how that impacts our parenting, we will now focus on what it means to build a foundation for your family. The Bible is clear about how our beliefs impact the actions we take in life. The question is, do you know what you believe and why you believe it? Even more, are you able to explain to your children what you believe? Do the choices and actions you take reflect those beliefs? Is your life something that your children would want to model?

Let us start with looking at what Jesus teaches about building a firm foundation. In verse twenty-one of Matthew 7 Jesus says only those who do the will of the Father will enter Heaven. What is the will of the Father, our God? Luke 10:27 answers this:

> *"You must love the Lord your God with all your heart, all your soul, all your strength, and all your mind and love your neighbor as yourself." Luke 10: 27 NLT*

What does this have to do with building a firm foundation? The way you live your life and what you teach your children will establish a foundation for your family that will help to lay the groundwork for the rest of their lives. There are three keys to building a firm foundation. These are what you believe, how you live your life and how you teach your children.

WHAT YOU BELIEVE

It is hard to establish a firm foundation if you do not know what you believe, and knowing what you believe is necessary to establish Biblical values in your children Both of our parents gave us the legacy of knowing what we believe and the importance of making those beliefs our own. It is one thing to have beliefs as parents and another to teach your children what you believe. They need to see it modeled, talked about, and evident in your actions so they can start to develop their own beliefs.

The foundation of our belief is:

- Jesus is God and that He came to earth to die for our sins.

> *"For this is how God loved the world: He gave his one and only Son, so that everyone who believes in him will not perish but have eternal life. God sent his Son into the world not to*

judge the world, but to save the world through him."
John 3:16-17 NLT

- Jesus was resurrected to demonstrate His power over death.

  "For since we believe that Jesus died and was raised to life again, we also believe that when Jesus returns, God will bring back with him the believers who have died."
  1 Thessalonians 4:14 NLT

- We as sinful people can receive Jesus's gift of salvation through acknowledging our sins, believing in Jesus and following Him.

  "For the wages of sin is death, but the free gift of God is eternal life through Christ Jesus our Lord."
  Romans 6:23 NLT

  "We are made right with God by placing our faith in Jesus Christ. And this is true for everyone who believes, no matter who we are. For everyone has sinned; we all fall short of God's glorious standard. Yet God, in his grace, freely makes us right in his sight. He did this through Christ Jesus when he freed us from the penalty for our sins. For God presented Jesus as the sacrifice for sin. People are made right with God when they believe that Jesus sacrificed his life, shedding his blood.

  Romans 3:22-25 NLT

  "If you openly declare that Jesus is Lord and believe in your heart that God raised him from the dead, you will be saved.

For it is by believing in your heart that you are made right with God, and it is by openly declaring your faith that you are saved."
Romans 10:9-10 NLT

- We show our love for God by showing His love to those around us.

  "And this is his commandment: We must believe in the name of his Son, Jesus Christ, and love one another, just as he commanded us."
  1 John 3:23 NLT

- One day He will return and take us into heaven and spend eternity with God.

  "For since we believe that Jesus died and was raised to life again, we also believe that when Jesus returns, God will bring back with him the believers who have died."
  1 Thessalonians 4:14 NLT

HOW YOU LIVE YOUR LIFE

Knowing what you believe is important. You need to be able to tell others what you believe, and it should drive the way that you live your life. I John 3:18 says this well:

  "Dear children, let's not merely say that we love each other; let us show the truth by our actions." I John 3:18 NLT

This is where most of us fail. We talk about what we believe, but our actions do not often reflect this. If you look at our bank accounts or our schedules you see that our lives are often filled with priorities based on what we want and not based on what God wants for us. We say we are followers of Jesus, but we find it hard to tithe our money. We live on our income for ourselves and give what we may have left over. But the Bible teaches that we should give first to Him and that He will provide what we need for the rest.

We talk about following Jesus, but how much time do we spend reading the Bible and talking to Him in prayer each day? We talk about loving our neighbor, but do we really show that we love people who are not like us? Do our kids see us giving our time and resources to those who are less fortunate?

This was an area that I had to work on. I was raised to know the truth of God's love and how to accept Jesus as my Savior, but it took me a long time to understand and live a life that was fully surrendered to Him. For much of my adult life, I compartmentalized each area of my life – this part was for God, another part was for my family, and some was for me. I thought if I were giving God His segment, I could do whatever I wanted with the rest. I learned that I was wrong. God wanted all of me, not just the portion I wanted to give. He wanted me to sacrifice control and trust Him. This took me a long time to figure out and do, but it has been so rewarding to live a life surrendered to Him. However, I did experience my share of pain along the journey to get there.

I was raised in an environment that talked about God and love, but often did not live this out. My home was filled with judgment against those who lived sinful lives and lacked acceptance of the fact that we are **all sinners**. There were classes of sin – some were accepted and not talked about, and others were judged. Lifestyles that were different from ours were judged and condemned, but gossip, envy and pride were often overlooked. Spiritual knowledge was valued over actions and the lives of the people in church were anything but attractive to those who were not part of the church family.

Your life reflects your true beliefs. You cannot claim to love others if you do not show that love in **what** you do.

HOW WE TEACH OUR CHILDREN

We must know what we believe, live out what we believe and lastly as parents we must teach our children what is right and wrong. Proverbs 22:6 says this well:

> *"Direct your children onto the right path, and when they are older, they will not leave it." Proverbs 22:6 NLT*

How well do you do this? Do you show your children what path they should follow, or do you leave that up to others, like teachers at school or in church or their friends? Do you spend time teaching your children about right and wrong and moral values in how they should live their life? In today's culture, society teaches our children that everything is okay if it feels right to you and that there are no moral rights and wrongs. But this type of teaching will lead our kids to trouble, potential great damage, and challenges in their life. We cannot neglect the importance of teaching our children and creating an open environment to ask questions and to learn what the Bible teaches about these things.

How do you teach your children? There are many ways to teach others, but it starts with being a learner yourself. You must study and learn. It is hard to teach others if you are not always seeking to learn yourself. You need to seek out the answer to your questions from the Bible and from other resources that help expand your knowledge and understanding. Being curious and wanting to know things is the best example to teach your kids. Help them to be curious and ask questions. When they ask, do not answer with because the Bible says so, but rather teach them how to find the answers for themselves by studying their Bible and seeing what it says. It is important that your children see you reading your Bible.

Another way to teach is to show your children how you spend your money and what you give back to God. Make giving a part of their routine by teaching them to give back to God whenever they earn money with allowances, chores, or side jobs. This is important to start at an early age so that they learn to make this a priority in their lives as well.

Take time to know what your children are being taught in their schools. Discuss what they are learning and give them time to ask questions and find out how what they are learning and how it may be different or the same from what you believe. You must ask questions of teachers, administrators as well as your kids to know what they are being taught. As a parent you are the most important teacher in your children's lives. Make it a priority!

These verses help lay out a pattern for your life. Love God, commit to the commands from the Bible and repeat them over and over and talk about them all the time.

"And you must love the Lord your God with all your heart, all your soul, and all your strength. And you must commit yourselves wholeheartedly to these commands that I am giving you today. Repeat them again and again to your children. Talk about them when you are at home and when you are on the road, when you are going to bed and when you are getting up."
Deuteronomy 6:5-7 NLT

These are just a few examples of ways to teach your children. We will talk about more ideas in the chapters to come. I want to close with this verse from Psalms 78:7:

"So each generation should set its hope anew on God, not forgetting his glorious miracles and obeying his commands."
Psalms 78:7 NLT

It is our role as parents to teach our children about God and His teachings to prepare them for the decision we hope each of our children will make to decide to follow Jesus for themselves. What can a firm foundation do for your family? It provides consistency, clarity, truth, and love. A basis for wisdom and making wise choices in their lives.

3 Keys to Building a Godly and Firm Foundation

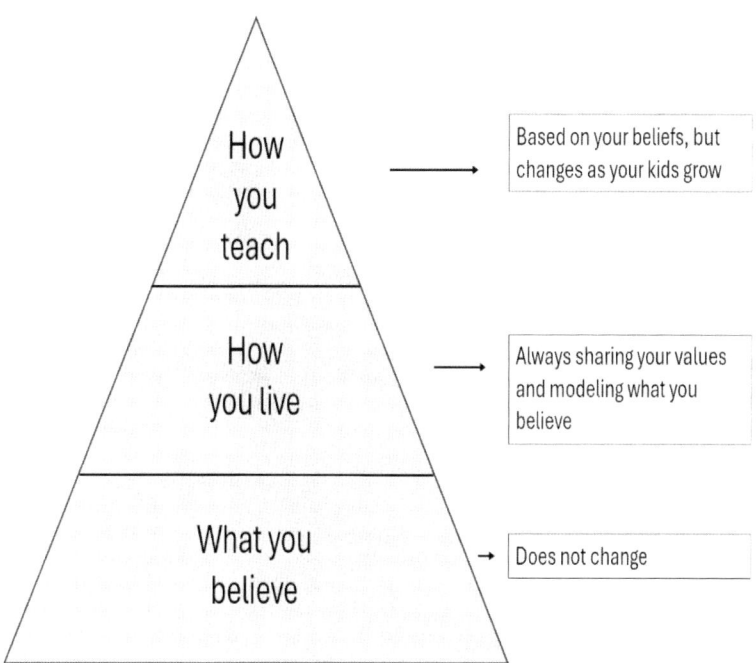

Reflection Questions:

- Would you say that your life is totally surrendered to Jesus? What steps do you need to take to surrender your life to Jesus?

- How well does your life model what you believe? Can others around you, including your children see that you model what you believe?

- What can you do to teach your children about God and how to develop a relationship with Jesus?

- How well are you able to tell your children what you believe and why?

Discussion Questions:

- Why is it important to teach your children?

- Why do you think Luke 10:27 is a good foundation for your family?

- What parenting advice do you learn from Matthew 7:21-27?

- What do you believe about Jesus?

- Why are our actions so important in parenting?

- What does 1 John 3:18 say that we should do? What are actions that show you love others?

- When you teach your children, which areas do you do well at and where do you want to improve?

- What is the hardest part of living out your faith in a way that teaches your children?

Prayer:

Write a prayer asking God to help you as you instill what you believe to your children. Ask Him to help you to model well and teach your children Godly values.

_____

_____

_____

_____

_____

_____

_____

_____

_____

_____

_____

_____

_____

_____

_____

_____

_____

_____

_____

_____

_____

_____

_____

_____

3 – MAKING CHURCH A PRIORITY

The first two chapters of this book were about laying a firm foundation. Now we will talk about the building blocks you lay on top of that foundation to help you build Godly children. We will look at values that you can use. These values will help you and your children to live Godly lives. In addition, they will help you have a fulfilling and healthy life now, and for their future families. These building blocks are things that we strive to attain, knowing we will make mistakes along the way. They create a pathway to establish healthy patterns and routines within the busyness that every family faces.

The first building block that we are going to talk about is making church a priority as a weekly rhythm in your home. In Hebrews 10:25 it says:

> *"And let us not neglect our meeting together, as some people do, but encourage one another, especially now that the day of his return is drawing near." Hebrews 10:25 NLT*

Church is a place of gathering. When I was young, the idea of going to church was a normal thing for most families. No matter what your church affiliation was, most people were of the mindset that they should go to church every week. It was a place where families would gather, and people usually were dressed in their finest clothes. Sunday was a day of rest, and most businesses were closed on Sundays so there were not as many distractions.

Today that is not the case. Most businesses are open on Sundays and there are sports activities and events that fill most family's calendars. Church attendance has been declining for many years as the events and activities on Sunday have replaced what used to be church time. After Covid and the shift to doing things online, even more people stopped making church attendance a regular activity. It became easier to watch a service online when the time was best for you, and you could stay in the comfort of your own home. Even as Covid stopped being an influence, many people never returned to the routine of attending church each week.

There is nothing wrong with watching church online, and it has many positive things that it has helped with, but there are some things that watching church online cannot do for you and your family. There are three key things that make attending church in a physical location an important building block for your family.

PLACE OF LEARNING

First, church is a place of learning for you and your family. A good church has great Biblical teaching for your own spiritual growth and should also provide teaching for children that is age appropriate and relevant to their learning style. Learning is enhanced when you do it with others, and you have leaders who will provide tools that help you take that teaching home with you. When you go to church together, you will have time together after church as you travel home or your next event to discuss what you learned with your family and how they should apply it to your lives. Plus, our children need to have more age-appropriate Biblical teaching to balance off what they are learning from school, other friends or on social media. Kids are influenced by what they observe, hear, and are taught. You need to make sure that you add learning from places like church that align with your family beliefs and values.

BUILDS RELATIONSHIPS

The second thing attending church does is help build relationships. Attending church gives you an opportunity to meet new people or make connections with existing friends. You get to see, connect with, and show engagement with people face to face. Our online worlds and social media have made it harder to establish and maintain personal connections where you can touch, make eye contact, and see body language which are all part of maintaining healthy lives and relationships. Also, your children get to make new friends or play together with existing friends in a safe and nurturing environment. Church friends may also be school friends that help them to expand their relationships. Church also is a place where you can build relationships with older adults who can help mentor and invest in your children. There may be small group leaders, class teachers or other adults who are your friends at church that they can interact with and learn from.

For us, most of our family friends have come from attending church. We met people who we became friends with and often did "life together" with. These friends had kids similar in age to our children and our families did things together. Most of these people we would never have met were we not attending church together.

SETS A PATTERN

The third thing that making church a priority does is to help build a pattern or routine in your family's life. Building routines are healthy. They help establish boundaries and patterns that can help children to feel safe and under control. Attending church together as a family creates time each week where everyone must be ready, travel to the same place and have shared experiences to talk about. It is something for people to look forward to and know what to expect each week. When you as parents set the example and make it a priority in your life, your children are being taught that this is something they should continue doing once they leave home and start their own families.

I know from experience that kids will complain about having to get ready and go to church. They say they do not want to go, but if you establish attending church at an early age, they will know that this is just part of what is expected of them. It is always harder to start a new routine and get people used to change than it is to start this before you have kids and continue it while they are young. There were weekends where I wanted to stay home rather than packing up the kids and taking them to church, but when I look back, I am glad that I did as I see my grown kids with their families doing the same.

There will always be times when you miss church, but you set the tone for how the family will view these times. When our kids were younger, we often spent many weekends away at a cabin. There was not a church that was close by so our kids asked to do "cabin church." One child would sing a song, one would take the offering and usually mom, dad or their grandparents would do a little sermon and one of the kids would pray to close. It did not have to be a normal church service, but it showed that our kids thought it was a priority and it gave them an opportunity to be involved.

The last element of setting a pattern is seeing the parents being involved at church by serving, and not just being attenders. We participated in our church and served in different roles during various stages of our lives. We were teachers, nursery volunteers and small group leaders. We served in positions of leadership when asked and made being involved in the ministries of the church a priority. Being involved showed our kids that church was more than just a place we attended every week, but a place that was part of our life and set a pattern for them as they grew older. Our kids continue to be involved in their church even though they now have families of their own.

Throughout this chapter I assumed that you were attending a church that taught Biblical values and that the teaching, worship, and kid's programs were engaging and relevant. I know sometimes the church we attend does not meet those expectations. I do not encourage going from church to church, but there are times when a change is needed. If you have done everything you can to encourage and help the church to change and nothing is happening, it may be time to find a place that will offer services that meet the needs of your family.

There was a time in our lives where we had to make that change. We attended the same church for many years and were actively involved in it. However, the preaching was becoming hard to learn from and we and our kids were complaining more about church than we were enjoying it. We made several efforts to lead change, but it was clear the pastor was not leading in the direction we hoped it would go. After many weeks of prayer and discussion, we decided to check out some different churches. On our first visit we found a church that had everything we were looking for and that our kids loved. We made the switch and never regretted it.

Church should be a place that you love to attend and bring life to you and your family. Jesus did not come to earth to create churches filled with rules and traditions. He came to create places that made a difference in people's lives and that were places of joy, community and caring for others.

Reflection Questions:

- Do you love attending your church? If not, what will it take to change your feelings about church so that your kids can see your love to attend church?

- What are the things that make attending church regularly difficult for you?

- What keeps you from making a church a priority in your life?

- What changes do you need to make to make church a priority in your life?

Discussion Questions:

- What does Hebrews 10:25 say is one of the benefits of attending church?

- What do you love about the church you attend? What do your children love about your church?

- Where could your church improve to make it a place that you and your kids would want to attend and invite friends to?

- What keeps you from making church a part of your weekly routine? Is it on your calendar so that you never miss it?

- Of the three reasons mentioned to make church a priority (place of learning, builds relationships, sets a pattern), which one is the most important to you and why? Which reason is the most challenging for you and why?

Prayer:

Write a prayer thanking God for His church and what you love about your church. Ask God to show you how you can help your children to be involved in church as they grow up.

_____

_____

_____

_____

_____

_____

_____

_____

_____

_____

_____

_____

_____

_____

_____

_____

_____

_____

_____

_____

_____

_____

4 -BUILDING CHILDREN WITH CHARACTER

The topic of building character could be an entire book by itself. It is something that every parent wants their child to have but it takes a lifetime to build, and one wrong decision can destroy it. Building character in your children starts with building character in yourself. That is what makes this so hard. Your children are always watching you. They hear what you say, but they almost always follow what you do. You cannot create expectations for your children that you do not live for yourself. Too often we say one thing for our kids to follow and we do something different for ourselves. Some examples you tell you kids:

- "You should watch less TV" - when we have the TV on all day ourselves.
- "You should read your Bible and pray" - but they never see us reading our Bibles or spending time in prayer.
- "You should say you are sorry to your brother for hitting him" - but we never say sorry when we lose our temper and yell.
- "Don't say those words" - when we use the same words in our conversations.

Children mirror the behaviors and actions that they see from their parents. When we are not disciplined or manage our spending wisely, how can we expect our children to do the same? You may feel like you have already made mistakes with your kids, but there is always an opportunity to start new and rebuild what you may have already damaged.

What does the Bible say about character? Here are a couple of verses:

> *"But the Lord said to Samuel, "Do not judge by his appearance or height, for I have rejected him. The Lord does not see things the way you see them. People judge by outward appearance, but the Lord looks at the heart.""*
> *1 Samuel 16:7 NLT*

> *"The godly walk with integrity; blessed are their children who follow them."*
> *Proverbs 20:7 NLT*

> *"Guard your heart above all else, for it determines the course of your life."*
> *Proverbs 4:23 NLT*

In this chapter we are going to talk about four aspects of character that are important to build in your children. They are honesty, responsibility, accountability, and forgiveness.

HONESTY

Telling the truth. Sounds so easy but it is much harder than you think. Children from an early age can sin and lie. When your child makes a mess in the house and you ask them "Who did this?" Their first response is to say, "Not me!" Why is it so easy to lie? There are many factors from fear of not wanting to get in trouble, to shame for what we did wrong, to rejection because we failed. Because these emotions can be so strong and influential in our lives, we choose not to tell the truth. Everyone knows that this is a problem. Our words are just a reflection of what is going on in our mind and our minds are sinful. As it says in Romans:

> *"For everyone has sinned; we all fall short of God's glorious standard."*
>
> *Romans 3:23 NLT*

How do we teach our kids to be honest when everything around them is pushing them in the opposite direction? We must teach wisdom. These verses from Psalms and Proverbs give us why this is important.

> *"But you desire honesty from the womb, teaching me wisdom even there."*
>
> *Psalms 51:6 NLT*
>
> *"Honesty guides good people; dishonesty destroys treacherous people."*
>
> *Proverbs 11:3 NLT*
>
> *"Truthful words stand the test of time, but lies are soon exposed."*
>
> *Proverbs 12:19 NLT*

Honesty is about being truthful, even when the truth hurts. It is learning that speaking truth and not lies is how to gain trust and respect from others. It is speaking the truth in love. If you want to hear the truth, then tell the truth. If you think you deserve to be told the truth, then do the same for others. When we are not honest, we show that we lack character. Dishonesty is when we do not care what others think about us and we do not care about them either. Their opinion does not matter.

Model honesty to your children. Our kids need to see us being honest to those we talk to. When we are dishonest with others, our kids learn that it really is okay to lie.

Where do we start?

- Teach your children to always speak the truth.

    "Those who lead blameless lives and do what is right, speaking the truth from sincere hearts."

    Psalms 15:2 NLT

    "Instead, we will speak the truth in love, growing in every way more and more like Christ, who is the head of His body, the church. Ephesians 4:15 NLT

- Teach your children that lying creates problems and challenges for them. A small lie often results in more and bigger lies to cover for the first lie. It is important to teach them that telling the truth is more important than what they did wrong. We all make mistakes, but your child needs to learn to always tell the truth instead of covering it up with a lie.

- Accept your children no matter what they have done. The fear of rejection is a powerful influence. Children often lie because they fear if they tell the truth, their behavior will cause them to be rejected. Our children need to see that they are valued and loved no matter what they have done.

RESPONSIBILITY

Teaching a child is challenging work, but we are told to do it. In Deuteronomy it says the following:

> *"Teach them to your children. Talk about them when you are at home and when you are on the road, when you are going to bed and when you are getting up."*
>
> *Deuteronomy 11:19 NLT*

This verse is referring to God's commands and truths, but they also apply to teaching responsibility to your children. You are always teaching - morning, night, home or away. Teaching your children responsibility is challenging. Often it is easier to do things ourselves than it is to get our kids to help. But when you do not teach this from an early age, it is much harder to change behaviors as they get older. Teaching responsibility is about giving children tasks and holding them accountable to completing them. Sometimes this may involve rewards but be careful to not make doing tasks always expecting a reward. When you give a task and you give a positive response when it is complete, you teach the behavior you want to develop. The child learns that what they have done made you happy and all children want to see that their behavior makes you happy. When something is not done to your expectations, be careful not to respond in anger because then you are teaching behavior that does things out of fear rather than motivating them to do it for the right reason – being responsible.

Let me give you a practical example. When you give your child a task to pick up the toys, tell them what is expected of them (pick up all the toys), what happens after they do it (play with something else) and give them the consequence of not doing the task (no more play time until a future time). Then if the child completes the task, show them your appreciation, and do whatever was promised as a reward. For example, the reward could be treated like a "High five" or a word of praise. If the task is not completed, then ensure that the consequence is given. Teaching responsibility takes work on our part. If you want to teach your children to be responsible, make sure your expectations are clear, success is defined and that you follow through on your commitments. In doing this we teach our children how to be responsible at an early age. We do this not because we are having them do the things we do not want to do, but rather to teach them that being responsible is how you gain trust and are rewarded with greater responsibilities in the future.

Unfortunately, if these skills have not been taught to you as a child, it can be extremely hard to change your behavior. However, with the right encouragement and support, any person can learn how to do this. No matter how old your children are today, start using these tools to help your children to learn how to be responsible. The older they are the harder the behavior may be to develop and will result in some conflict because your expectations have changed, and they have learned what they can get away with already.

Teach your children that every person matters. God created all of us, and we all matter to God.

> *"So God created human beings in His own image. In the image of God He created them; male and female He created them. Genesis 1:27 NLT*

ACCOUNTABILITY

Accountability comes from learning honesty and responsibility. It is the combination of these two attributes.

> *"If you are faithful in little things, you will be faithful in large ones. But if you are dishonest in little things, you will not be honest with greater responsibilities."*
>
> *Luke 16:10 NLT*

When a person is accountable, their words and actions are trustable. They do what they say they will do, and they are honest when they do not complete it in the way that was expected. Accountability reflects being able to demonstrate both the skill and the responsibility to get things done without your requiring monitoring or supervision.

Let us go back to the last example of cleaning up toys. When you first ask your child to do this task, you watch them, make sure they put things in the proper place, and you coach them along the way. Accountability comes with the completion of the same tasks a second or third time. The child knows when you say to clean up the toys, what should be cleaned up and where things go. You do not need to be present to coach or help along the way and they complete the task again. In time your child learns that they can be trusted to do things they have been asked to and they will complete them as expected.

As your children grow older, what they are trusted with expands as they demonstrate their accountability to manage responsibilities. This is as simple as knowing the rules and trusting them to live by the rules. As children show they are honest and responsible, they earn greater trust because they have proven to be accountable. As the parent, it is our job to ensure that the expectations are clearly explained. Conflict comes when you expect one thing, but that expectation was not clearly explained, communicated, or understood.

Let me share an example from my family. When our children were teenagers, we had a clear expectation that there was to be no drinking of alcohol in our house by them or their friends. Our son had a party at our house and invited friends over. One of his friends brought cans of beer in his pockets. Our son knew the rules, so he told his friend that alcohol was not allowed in our house and that he would have to get rid of the beer or leave. His friend was upset, but our son held his ground and the friend left. This demonstrated accountability by our son.

FORGIVENESS

The last element of character is one of the hardest to teach and model. We all make mistakes or poor choices. That is a reality. The question of character is what we do when we make a mistake.

"Make allowance for each other's faults, and forgive anyone who offends you. Remember, the Lord forgave you, so you must forgive others." Colossians 3:13

Teaching our kids to be honest, responsible, and accountable also means they need to admit when they make mistakes and seek forgiveness from the person that they hurt. That is the first step, but the second part is often even harder and that is to forgive the person who did something to hurt or harm you. In the Bible, Jesus was asked how often you should forgive someone:

"Then Peter came to him and asked, "Lord, how often should I forgive someone who sins against me? Seven times?" "No, not seven times," Jesus replied, "but seventy times seven!" Matthew 18:21-22 NLT

Jesus responded by saying not seven times but seventy times seven (that is 490 for those who struggle with math). It is not about how many times you forgave, but rather it is about always being willing to forgive.

In the Bible it says that we have all sinned and that when we ask forgiveness for our sins they are forgiven and washed away.

"But if we confess our sins to Him, He is faithful and just to forgive us our sins and to cleanse us from all wickedness." I John 1:9 NLT

Our children learn this truth often based on how we as parents live it out. When our kids have done something wrong, how do we respond? Do we accept their forgiveness and forget about it? Or do we say we forgive them, but the next time they do something we remind them of their past mistakes and keep track of all the wrongs they have done. All too often this is how we respond. We remind them of their past mistakes and do not demonstrate true forgiveness by forgetting about it.

The other side is also true. We as parents make mistakes too. We lose our temper and get angry, but then do not go back and ask our children for forgiveness. I never remember my dad ever asking for forgiveness when he lost control. As we started to raise our children, I was repeating this pattern. I would set down the rules and enforce their adherence. When my son did not do what I had told him to do, I lost my temper and responded in anger to him. As I was telling Beth about what was going on, she asked me a simple question. "Is it worth it? Are you willing to lose your relationship with your son over trying to be right?" It broke my heart because I realized at that point, I was becoming my father. I went to my son and apologized to him for my behavior. It broke my sinful pride at having to be right and it saved my relationship with all my children. He accepted my apology and we started to get along better. I still made mistakes and still lost my temper, but I remembered two things, seek forgiveness and even more importantly, prioritize my response to avoid losing my temper in the first place.

One note on this topic. I am referencing normal conflicts in relationships. I am not talking about abusive relationships. When danger and intentional harm is done, there is a place for forgiveness but not always for forgetting. We should work towards being able to forgive people for what they have done to you, but that does not mean that you do not set boundaries or other types of barriers to protect yourself from potential future abusive behaviors.

Reflection Questions:

- Are there things that you have done that you need to seek forgiveness for? Jot down what comes to your mind.

- Are there things that you need to "let go" to show others that you have truly forgiven them?

- Are there parts of your own character that you need to work on?

Discussion Questions:

- What is character to you? How would define someone who has character?

- What areas of character do you struggle with the most? Honesty, responsibility, accountability, or forgiveness? What do you need to improve in your own life?

- What tips do you have on how to teach responsibility to your kids?

- Under the section on teaching your children to be honest, which point do you need to work on?

- What are ways you teach honesty to your children?

- How do you teach your children to be responsible?

- Why do you think teaching children to be accountable is important?

- Are there character traits beyond the four mentioned here that you think is important to teach your children and why?

- Share a time that you had to ask your child for forgiveness.

Prayer:

Write a prayer asking God to reveal and examine your heart. Ask Him to help you as you instill honesty, responsibility, accountability, and forgiveness in your children.

_____

_____

_____

_____

_____

_____

_____

_____

_____

_____

_____

_____

_____

_____

_____

_____

_____

_____

_____

_____

_____

_____

_____

_____

5 - DISCIPLINING YOUR CHILDREN

"Those who spare the rod of discipline hate their children. Those who love their children care enough to discipline them."
Proverbs 13:24 NLT

One of the most challenging things about being a parent is learning how to discipline your children. Every child is different, but in each stage of growing up, they are learning. They are learning language skills, relationship skills and behavior skills. Our role as parents is learning how to teach them in every area.

When it comes to behavior skills, it is the parent's job to teach what is right and wrong and that there are consequences to their choices. How children learn about behavior is influenced by the world they live in. With our society continuing to move away from moral teaching, it will become increasingly more important to emphasize discipline and setting morals in the home.

The Bible gives us clear expectations and examples of how we should live and what we view as right and wrong. Reading in the Bible is one thing, but enforcing those boundaries and consequences is much more challenging. Usually in a marriage, one parent is the strict one and one is more of the loving or accepting parent. In our family, I was the strict one who usually set and enforced the rules and Beth was more of a loving and caring person. This did not mean that I could not be loving and caring, and Beth could not enforce discipline, but we each had our natural tendencies.

During our time of raising children, we found these four guidelines helped us navigate disciplining our children. They were: Be consistent, punishment matches the offense, never discipline in anger, and use discipline as a teaching moment.

BE CONSISTENT

One of the most important aspects of teaching your children is to be consistent. This is true in all aspects of teaching, but especially when it comes to teaching behavior. As a parent, you must apply the same rules and expectations to each child in your family and enforce them in the same way. If you allow a bad behavior one time and not another, your children are not being taught discipline. It does not establish a clear boundary for them and will create more confusion and potentially more challenging behavior in the future.

As children get older, they are always challenging boundaries to see what they can get away with. Setting clear boundaries when they are young will help you when you deal with them as they become teenagers. The boundaries you are trying to enforce for teenagers become more impactful with greater consequences if they are crossed.

Parenting and discipline are a lot like a river that flows through the countryside. The water in the river flows downstream because the flow is controlled by the banks of the river. The banks keep the water contained and flowing in the direction you want it to. When a storm comes or you have melting from winter, the flow of the water increases and without high enough banks to keep the water flowing, it will overflow the banks and cause flooding.

Our job as parents is to build these banks that our children will be growing up with so that when the floods come, such as peer pressure, or moral challenges, our children will be better protected from the damage that could be caused by those floods. Will you stop all the floods from happening? No, but the more you have built a firm foundation and established the framework for decision making in your kids, they will have a better chance to resist temptation and make wise choices in their lives. When they make mistakes, and they will, our job is to use discipline to help our children understand the consequences of their choices.

A second part of being consistent is working together as parents to establish what the banks of the river are and enforce them consistently. Children seem to learn that usually one parent will say "no" so they ask the other parent to see if they can get what they want. As parents you must work hard to communicate with each other, so that you are consistent about boundaries and how to discipline. An example would be a child going to his dad and asking if they could have a cookie. When the dad says "no" they go to mom and mom says "yes." Asking for a cookie is a minor thing, but the pattern teaches the kids to ask the other parent when one says no. As a parent, we must learn to ask "Did you already ask dad for a cookie? What did he say?" And then ask dad if what you are told was accurate. If dad said no, then mom needs to say no too. If mom disagrees with dad's answer, she needs to talk with dad and talk about it and if the decision is changed, dad should say yes and why he changed his decision. This may sound like a lot of work for something as minor as a cookie, but it is being consistent that we are striving to teach.

It is always best to talk through these scenarios as spouses and decide how you want to answer or set the boundaries before you in that situation, and it can cause conflict. Being prepared and working towards agreement as spouses will help you be consistent with your children in a healthy way.

PUNISHMENT MATCHES THE CRIME

How you choose to discipline is a challenging part of parenting. Each parent comes from a different past and how they were disciplined as children will impact the way they discipline as a parent. There are many resources that talk about how to discipline your children and the form of punishment you should use. I am not advocating one form of discipline over another. I want to encourage you to make sure that the form of discipline that is used relates to the severity of the action that resulted in the punishment needing to be taken.

For example, when one of your children hits a sibling or a friend, disciplining them with spanking does not match the offense. When a child hits, by choosing to punish with spanking the child, the punishment uses the same technique (hitting) as the offense. This sends the wrong message that hitting is okay.

There are behaviors that have different levels of discipline that are needed as consequences for that behavior. Some behaviors are normal childhood challenges and others are more serious and need to be addressed before they get out of control.

The other key factor is the temperament of your child. Discipline impacts each child differently and what has a significant impact on one may be different for another one. As a parent it is important to apply discipline based on what will make an impact on the child the most and what their emotional state is. For example, sending a very social child to their room for a timeout may be very impactful because they are losing the social interaction with others while an introverted child might not be impacted by sending them to their room because they like the alone time.

Discipline is usually about taking away something of value or importance for whatever time fits with what the behavior was. These things will change as a child gets older and the amount of time you enforce discipline will change as well. For a toddler, the discipline may be a one-minute time out away from playing. A general guideline is the timeout should vary with their age. One year old is one-minute, two-year-old is two-minutes, a three-year-old is three-minutes, etc. For a teenager it may be no TV or Internet for two days.

NEVER DISCIPLINE IN ANGER

This should be an easy guideline, but it is so much harder to do in the moment of discipline. We have the most potential to incur lasting negative impact on our children when we discipline in anger. Our children often confuse the pain they receive as a rejection from the parent rather than a consequence for their actions. We also are more inclined to punish more harshly when we are angry.

So how do you avoid punishing your child out of anger? Here are three steps:

- Give yourself a timeout. When something is done by your child that makes you angry, step away from the situation to allow yourself time to avoid responding in anger and saying or doing something you may regret later. Take a thirty second cooling down break before you say or do anything.
- Seek advice from your spouse or trusted friend before acting. Let them help you talk through the situation to ensure the discipline is appropriate based on what happened.
- Explain your actions to the child before you give them the discipline so that they understand how it applies to what they did.

Always remember, if you lose it and respond out of anger, go back, and apologize later after you cool down and realize what you did. This reinforces what I talked about in Chapter 4 on teaching your children about forgiveness.

USE AS A TEACHING MOMENT

As a parent you are always teaching. Sometimes we teach as ways to prepare and guide our children and other times we teach out of their mistakes and related discipline. The goal is to help build Godly children who are wise and who can make good decisions when they are on their own and eventually raise their own children.

The book of Proverbs in the Bible is a great place to learn wisdom to teach yourself and your family. love this verse:

> *"If you reject discipline, you only harm yourself; but if you listen to correction, you grow in understanding."*
> *Proverbs 15:32 NLT*

This is one of the goals when raising your children. You want them to grow in understanding so that they can make wise choices.

Discipline is about teaching your children about the impact of their decisions and providing understanding, not punishment. We do not discipline our children to punish them, but rather to teach them. As parents, it is so important that we learn to be good teachers of expectations, so that when our child does something that violates those expectations, they understand the impact of the discipline they receive. Do not wait to teach your children about behavior expectations until after they do something that you think is wrong. Set the expectations or banks of the river first, and then discipline only when those expectations are broken. Do not expect your children to understand the rules if you have never told them what they are.

> *"No discipline is enjoyable while it is happening—it is painful! But afterward there will be a peaceful harvest of right living for those who are trained in this way."*
> *Hebrews 12:11 NLT*

Discipline is challenging work. It can be stressful and challenging and at times you may want to give up and stop trying. But you must remember why you are doing it. Discipline is to train and prepare your children for their future and the challenging work is done to help them have a successful and productive adult life. You are helping them to avoid difficulties and hardships that they could have avoided with the right teaching and discipline.

Reflection Questions:

- Think about your childhood – what discipline did you receive from your parents and how has it impacted how you discipline your children?

- How well have you done at setting clear behavior expectations for your children?

- Do you feel you and your spouse are consistent in how you discipline? If not, how have you worked out being consistent with your kids?

- Have you ever disciplined your kids when you were angry? Did you go back and apologize later?

Discussion Questions:

- What have you found to be helpful as your discipline your kids?

- How do you provide a teaching moment when you discipline your kids?

- How have you provided good banks of the river for your children as they have grown up?

- How have you adjusted your discipline based on the emotional make-up of your child?

Prayer:

Write a prayer asking God to help you as you discipline your children. Ask Him for wisdom and discernment as you shape your children through discipline.

_____

_____

_____

_____

_____

_____

_____

_____

_____

_____

_____

_____

_____

_____

_____

_____

_____

_____

_____

_____

_____

_____

_____

_____

6 – BE AN ENCOURAGER

Words matter! How we use them can have a significant impact on people's lives, especially our kids. In the Bible it says:

> *"So encourage each other and build each other up, just as you are already doing."*
> *1 Thessalonians 5:11 NLT*

> *"Do not use foul or abusive language. Let everything you say be good and helpful, so that your words will be an encouragement to those who hear them."*
> *Ephesians 4:29 NLT*

> *"Indeed, we all make many mistakes. For if we could control our tongues, we would be perfect and could also control ourselves in every other way."*
> *James 3:2 NLT*

Our children need to hear words of encouragement to help them to become the people that God designed them to be. Our words can either build them up or tear them down. Children are different, and they need encouragement in separate ways. Girls need to be encouraged by pointing out their inner beauty and boys need to be encouraged by recognizing their potential and pushing them to reach that potential.

I was raised in a home built around sarcasm. I have learned that sarcasm can be one of the worst ways to communicate because sarcasm is humor built around a little bit of truth. It is used to generate laughter at the expense of another person. Since this is how my father communicated, this is also how I learned to communicate. To make people laugh I would say something to generate a laugh at somebody else's expense. In my family growing up that was usually my siblings, but it could also be used towards my parents since that was allowed and seemed to be okay to do.

When I got married, I continued this style, only this time the humor was directed towards Beth. In my heart, I meant nothing bad by it, but what I did not realize was how much my words hurt Beth and made her feel like a failure. Most often this occurred in activities with our friends, and it took a long time for me to connect our conflicts with my words. When Beth finally told me how my words were impacting her, I learned that I needed to change. It is challenging work to change the behavior that you have, but over the years I have learned to use my words better. I am always striving to be an encourager instead of a critic now.

Here are three ways to be an encourager: See the good in people; be a good listener; and encourage the dreams of others.

SEE THE GOOD IN PEOPLE

Can you think of someone in your life who is always complaining or making negative comments about every person, experience or place they interact with? How much do you want to be around that person? Now think of someone who always makes you feel better about yourself when you spend time with them. Don't you want to spend as much time as possible with them? With that being the case, why are we not more encouraging and see the good in people? First, it has to do with our own insecurities. When we point out the negatives in others, we give the false impression that we are better than them. Seeing the good in people takes time and focus. So here is the challenge – focus on seeing three good things in every person or situation before you point out a negative. With our kids we talk about three pats on the back before we do one critique or criticism. It is easier to see what is wrong or what could be changed than it is to see what good is in the person or situation. But take it a step further. Do not just notice the good things but take the time to tell them about the good you saw in them. For example, when was the last time you went to a restaurant and got great service? Did you tell the manager about it? If you have bad service, I am sure it would be easy to tell them about that.

Something that we have started doing in our family is sharing one word of encouragement for the person that has a birthday ending in five or zero. Each person attending writes one word that they think positively describes the person on a sheet of paper and then we go around in a circle and each person gives their sheet with the word written on to the birthday person and explains why they picked that word. It is a small way to create an environment of seeing the good in people and sharing it with them and others.

Learning to affirm your children is so important. Our children need to hear that we believe in them and that they can accomplish anything they put their minds to. Parents need to be the biggest encouragers in their children's lives because if we do not encourage them, they will search for affirmation from someone else.

BE A GOOD LISTENER

"Understand this, my dear brothers and sisters: You must all be quick to listen, slow to speak, and slow to get angry."
James 1:19 NLT

You have two ears and one mouth for a reason! We need to learn to listen more and speak less. The reason that we are not good encouragers is because we are not good listeners. So often we spend more time and energy trying to get people to listen to us and our ideas that we forget to take the time to listen and hear the other person. Being listened to is one of the greatest ways to encourage somebody. We all have a desire to be heard, and when we are it makes us feel encouraged.

Beth was always good at this with our kids. When they would come home from school, she would sit down with them and listen to their day. What were their highlights, what were their challenges, and what did they do? That time was a way to encourage them and hear about things that she could help them with. That helped create open lines of communication especially as they moved into the teenage years. They always knew mom was there to listen and encourage them.

A second part of being a good listener is to remember. When your kids or others share information with you, do you remember what they said? Sometimes we take the time to listen, but we fail to take a mental note of what was being shared by them. One of the best ways to show encouragement to someone is to remember what they shared and then the next time you see them ask them about it. Remembering the topic, asking about what is new with that topic and listening to their response is a huge encouragement and shows that you genuinely care about them.

LET THEM DREAM

Have you ever sat down with a 4- or 5-year-old and asked them what they want to be or do when they grow up? Usually, they have wild ideas and big dreams. But what happens when you ask that same child ten years later? Those dreams become smaller, and they often have nothing big in life they are aiming for. Why is that? As parents we often do not do an excellent job of encouraging our kids to dream. We fill them with a sense of reality. We say things like, "you cannot do that or that is not possible." This discouragement will stop them from dreaming. This is often because we have lost focus on our own dreams, and it is hard to let our kids dream when we have no dreams for ourselves.

Our job as parents is to help our children unlock their dreams and remove the limitations, we put on them. Is it not true that we feel most fulfilled when we are pursuing our dreams? Why do we limit our children's dreams or try to put our dreams (or lack of them) on them? I always had the dream that one of my kids would be a star athlete and the captain of the team. Was that my kids dream? No! But I had to learn to let go of my dreams for them because they were not their dreams. That was hard at first, but I realized that they would only be doing it because I wanted it for them, and I realized I had to let it go. Now they all love sports and in hindsight it gave me more time to play in our yard with them growing up.

How do we help our kids unlock their dreams? Here are a few ideas. First, ask them about their dreams and do not make any limiting comments. We kill a lot of dreams because we critique an idea and point out why they could never do that.

A second idea is to give them an opportunity to make a dream become a reality. Let them produce an idea within what parameters you define and help them make that dream become a reality. One thing we did with our kids was allow them to plan a trip with me for their 13th birthday. They came up with the idea, planned the trip and my job was to make it happen. This was a small way to teach them that dreams are possible.

A third idea is to never stop dreaming yourself. The Bible is filled with stories of characters who received dreams from God and then spent their lives making those dreams become a reality. Examples are Joseph, Moses, Daniel, Nehemiah, and Peter. We are never too old to dream and to listen to what dreams God has for us. The most fulfilling thing in life is to know that we are spending our time and energy working towards our God-sized and God-given dreams. Our children are inspired to see us live out these dreams in our lives with Potential Endeavors and our work in Ukraine.

The last point is to give yourself and your kids time to dream. We are all so programmed and busy in our schedules and activities that we often have little quiet time to sit, listen and dream. Turn off the TV, put down your phone, say no to that coffee meeting, stop playing video games and spend time dreaming. Quiet time builds creativity, unlocks dreams, and resets your soul. Make it a priority to do it yourself and have your kids do the same and then share your dreams with each other.

Reflection Questions:

- When was the last time you shared words of encouragement with your kids?

- Do you use sarcasm in your home? How does that impact your family?

- What could you change or do that would help you to see the positive or good in others?

- How are your listening skills? When was the last time you were intentional to just listen and not share your opinion or thoughts?

- What are your kids' dreams? When was the last time you asked them?

- What are your dreams?

Discussion Questions:

- What do you do to encourage your children?

- What are your dreams for the future? How have you encouraged your children to dream and reach their full potential?

- What makes it hard to encourage your children?

Prayer:

Write a prayer asking God to help you encourage your children that is specific to their gifts and talents. Ask God to help you see the good in them, to be a good listener and to help your children to dream.

_____

_____

_____

_____

_____

_____

_____

_____

_____

_____

_____

_____

_____

_____

_____

_____

_____

_____

_____

_____

_____

_____

_____

_____

7 – MANAGING CONFLICT

Conflict is one of the things we have in our lives at one time or another but is also something that most people do not like dealing with. We try to avoid it and hope that it will go away or avoid it all together. However, managing conflict is something that is important to teach your children. Children are always watching you and how you deal with conflict, within your family, and with those outside your family. What you model will teach them how they should manage conflict themselves.

For me, conflict has never been something I have tried to avoid and have often found myself in the middle of it more often than I would like. However, what has changed over the years is how I respond to conflict and how I try to deal with it. Growing up and as a young adult I did not manage it well. I had issues with anger and pride. I loved to argue and would often not stop until I won the battle. My response and my pride created wounds and difficulties in friendships and my marriage. To be honest, I struggled with the need to always be right and was not good at accepting responsibility.

I have learned that part of my problem was anger and pride. This was what I learned from my father, and I was just repeating the same pattern in my life. I also had to do work to understand what was at the root of my anger and pride issues. As it says in Proverbs:

> *"Pride leads to conflict; those who take advice are wise."*
> *Proverbs 13:10 NLT*

It is important to teach our kids about pride as it is often the core root of all sin in our lives.

Why did I need to always be right? I go into more detail about this in my book <u>Swallowed by a Whale Twice</u>, but it involved an inner feeling of not being accepted and always being an outsider that needed to prove myself. It showed itself by being a workaholic and trying to show that I was the smartest and hardest working person. I liked to be in control of everything. It gave me success in the eyes of the world, but I was masking the real problem that that I needed to fix.

I had to learn that in God's eyes I was enough. I did not need to prove myself to others, but that God loved and accepted me as I was. My anger and pride came because of my feelings of failure. As I learned how to turn them over to God and accept who He created me to be, I became a different person. It did not happen overnight, but it was an evolving change. As I let go of control, my inner spirit began to change, and I became much more a reflection of the fruits of the spirit found in Galatians:

> *"But the Holy Spirit produces this kind of fruit in our lives: love, joy, peace, patience, kindness, goodness, faithfulness,"* Galatians 5:22 NLT

Why did I share this information about me in a chapter on managing conflict? Most of the conflict that happens in this world comes from sin. It involves pride, anger, control, entitlement, or false truth. Managing conflict is learning to look deeper than the specifics and understand the root cause of the problem. Learning how to deal with this issue is important in your own walk with God, but also in how you raise your kids and teach them.

I am going to share six tips to effectively manage conflict. They will give you a model to use whether in your family or in relationships outside of your home or even work.

1. OWN YOUR OWN PART

When you have conflict with someone, whether that is your child, spouse, or someone else, start by asking yourself what is **your** part that contributed to this conflict. Take a step back before you respond and ask yourself what **you** did and what **you** could have done differently. Conflicts escalate because we often respond before we think. Taking a breath and looking at yourself first is a safe way to slow down conflict or anger.

"Make allowance for each other's faults and forgive anyone who offends you. Remember, the Lord forgave you, so you must forgive others."
Colossians 3:13 NLT

2. ASK QUESTIONS

The second step is asking questions to seek understanding about the situation. Why are you upset? What did I do that made you upset? What were you hoping would happen? What can I do to resolve the conflict? Seeking to understand the situation rather than making comments or statements will always reduce the volatility of the situation.

3. BE SPECIFIC

Do not talk in general terms or absolutes. For example, do not say "You always do this!" or "Everybody feels this way!" Ask for specific examples and be specific about your own feelings. When you do this (whatever the specific issue is) this is how it makes me feel. Being specific helps to get at what is really the problem (the root cause) and what needs to be resolved to help it to go away.

4. ATTACK THE PROBLEM, NOT THE PERSON

In conflict situations, we often use words that attack the person rather than the problem. Work hard to avoid doing that. Do not say that they are a bad person or use adjectives that are negative toward the person. These comments are personal and attack them as individual instead of what the issue is. Personal attacks often make it harder to move back into a relationship with that person when the problem is resolved. This happens all the time in our current world. When someone has a different opinion on a topic than you do, we often decide the person is bad. We see this in politics and across social media. People are attacking the person rather than discussing the ideas. Our world needs more discussion and understanding why people share the opinions they have and less judgement towards the character of the person.

5. BE POSITIVE

Express that you want to see the problem resolved and the relationship restored. Believe the best in the other person and they also want to see the issue resolved. Many times, the problem is made worse by the assumptions we make, and our own human nature often goes to the negative rather than the positive. We usually assume the worst. We should assume the best and work towards resolving the issue. Are there bad people in the world? Yes! Are there evil people? Yes! Most people are not evil or have bad intentions. Most are just misunderstood, lonely, dealing with trauma or hurt in their past and just want to be loved and accepted for who they are.

> *"Instead, be kind to each other, tenderhearted, forgiving one another, just as God through Christ has forgiven you." Ephesians 4:32 NLT*

Forgiveness is a major theme of Jesus' life. He came to offer forgiveness to all who will accept it through His death and resurrection. His life is an example of what He did for us, and He wants us to do that for others.

6. PRAY

The last step is the most important. Ask the person how you can pray for them and what will be needed to resolve the conflict. It is hard to be mad at someone who is praying for you, and it is hard for you to pray when you are mad at someone else. If we would stop and pray at the beginning rather than as the last step, we may be able to avoid many of the hurts that come from the conflict.

> *"Confess your sins to each other and pray for each other so that you may be healed. The earnest prayer of a righteous*

person has great power and produces wonderful results. "
James 5:16 NLT

In summary, work towards showing love to each other. As it says in the Colossians,

"Above all, clothe yourselves with love, which binds us all
together in perfect harmony."
Colossians 3:14 NLT

I have talked about managing conflict and have not been specific about how this works with your children. That is because the principles work with children, but they learn more about how to manage conflict with others by watching you manage situations than by what happens between you and them. Many adults have unresolved conflicts with their parents or a sibling that have never been resolved. Families have avoided dealing with the issues that caused the conflict in the first place and it results in a separation that continues through the years.

Our children have been able to see how I worked on my issues and what Beth did with hers and it has resulted in a stronger relationship with our children and in how they want to resolve issues within their families as well.

Reflection Questions:

- How are you managing conflict in your life?

- Do you have any unresolved conflicts in your life that you need to deal with? If yes, what are you going to do to resolve it?

- Are there areas of your life that need to be worked on to help you with dealing with conflict? If yes, what is your first step to move forward?

- Does your life reflect the fruits of the spirit? If not, what is one area that you would like to work on to get better at?

- How are you praying for those you have conflicts with? Ask God to reveal to you any unresolved conflicts that you need to deal with and act on them!

Discussion Questions:

- Of the six tips for managing conflict, which is the hardest for you to do? And why?

- Share an example of how you have managed conflict with your children.

- How has pride caused you to have conflicts in your life?

Prayer:

Write a prayer asking God to help you deal with conflict with your children, spouse, and others. Ask Him to help you to own your part, to ask more questions, to get to the root of the conflict, to be clear, specific, and positive. Lastly, ask God to help you turn to prayer first in conflict.

_____

_____

_____

_____

_____

_____

_____

_____

_____

_____

_____

_____

_____

_____

_____

_____

_____

_____

_____

_____

_____

_____

_____

8 – HAVING FUN TOGETHER

Why couldn't the bicycle stand up by itself? It was two-tired. (HA! HA!) Laughter and having fun are great. There is something about having fun and laughing together that makes hard things seem to go away and you feel better about yourself and everything going on around you. The Bible says we should be filled with laughter and joy because of what God has done for us.

> *"We were filled with laughter, and we sang for joy. And the other nations said, "What amazing things the Lord has done for them." Psalms 126:2 NLT*

> *"A cheerful heart is good medicine, but a broken spirit saps a person's strength."*
> *Proverbs 17:22 NLT*

The thing about having fun together is that it is contagious. Fun and laughter are something that happens most often in groups. When one person has fun and laughs it is contagious and the people around them join in and it builds. If you want to have more fun and laugh more, do the following things.

MAKE TIME TOGETHER A PRIORITY

Our society has become more individualistic. We spend more time alone. We are entertained by watching TV or being on our phones using some form of social media. When Covid hit we were forced into isolation and people had to communicate at a distance, through windows or not at all.

Our schedules are busy. We have online remote jobs, kids go to on-line remote schools, we eat our meals at fast food restaurants. These things do not promote spending time together. People are exhausted by the busyness and demands on their time. It is your job as a parent to make spending time together a priority. Put it on the schedule. Turn off the TV and put away the phones. It does not necessarily matter what you do together, it is intentional planning to have a time when everyone is together that counts. Children may complain about wanting to be with their friends. Parents may have twenty-five other things that they feel they should be doing, but it does not matter. Put them all down and hang out together. In time laughter will happen. Someone will say something or do something that one of you laughs at and it will start. Give it a try!

DO FUN THINGS TOGETHER

Now that you have set aside a dedicated time to be together, plan some fun activities. Share the responsibility of planning activities with everyone in the family. Let each person choose what you will do, and everyone participates. It might be going to a park to play, playing in snow during the winter, going to a beach to swim in the summer, taking a family walk together, going to get ice cream. The list can go on and on. Again, it does not matter what you choose to do, it is the act of planning something and doing it together that matters. As you do things, I guarantee something will happen that someone will find funny and start to laugh. For our family that often involves spilling something down the front of a shirt. It is not planned; it just happens, and everyone will laugh at it and that just makes the experience more memorable. It also creates a lasting memory that you will talk about for years to come.

One thing we do with our grandkids is have "Dance Parties." We play a song, and we all dance along. Sometimes we get glow sticks, turn off the lights and dance around the house together. It is simple crazy fun that anyone can do and there are no rules or expectations other than to just have fun,

PLAY GAMES TOGETHER

Going out and doing things together is important, but playing games together is an important thing you can do together as a family. Playing games teaches things beyond just having fun. It teaches children how to follow rules, how to play together with others for shared or individual success and how to win or lose without getting mad. Being competitive can be a good learning tool for children as they grow up. They need to learn that if they win or lose it does not matter. The goal is to have fun!

The games you play will change as the children grow up but make it a priority to start and make it a family priority when they are young. When you play games together, things will happen that will make people laugh. It will remind you of past experiences that will often get people laughing. In our family, playing games always results in memories of playing games with family members. We often laugh about how Beth's grandma would play a game where she would bid by putting her finger out and then she would change her bid when she saw what everyone else was bidding. My mom always liked to eat snacks when she played games. And now we laugh about how my son always likes to make up new rules to the game we are playing to make it better.

Playing games may be a be a bedtime routine. You play one game together before they go to bed. It might be a game night. One night a week the calendar is scheduled for the family to play games together. Every family will be different, and it does not matter what games you play or how you incorporate them into your plans, it is important to be available to play games together.

To build Godly kids, it is important that they understand the importance of community and doing things together as a family and with other people. Fun and laughter come out of experiences, and it is what builds a bond between people. These things do not just happen. They take intentionality and planning.

Reflection Questions:

- What can you do to bring more joy into your family's life?

- How would you assess your ability to have fun together as a family?

- What are things that you want to start doing more of with your children?

Discussion Questions:

- What are the fun things you love to do as a family?

- What are your favorite games to play together as a family?

- What is a memory you have of when you were together with family and laughed uncontrollably?

Prayer:

Write a prayer asking God to help you incorporate more fun into your family. Ask Him to help you to make spending time together as a family a priority and to look for ways to have fun together.

_____

_____

_____

_____

_____

_____

_____

_____

_____

_____

_____

_____

_____

_____

_____

_____

_____

_____

_____

_____

_____

_____

_____

9 – HAVING MEALTIMES TOGETHER

Eating meals together is one of the areas that have changed the most since I was a child. When I was younger, it was normal to have meals together as a family. We did not eat fast food, and most meals were home cooked. It was a time when the whole family would be together, and we would spend an hour together. This was usually the evening meal, except on Sunday when it would be at lunchtime after church. We would all sit down, open with a prayer and eat whatever mom made for us. After dinner mom or dad would read the Bible and share a devotion with us. As we got older, we took turns doing devotions and we would end in a time of prayer. Then two of us would do the dishes and clean up from the meal.

Mealtimes were one of the things that I believe my parents did well. I have shared plenty about things they did not do as well, but this was one thing that they made a priority. At this meal we would share about our days and talk together. Often someone would tell a story and we would all laugh together. It was one of the best memories of my childhood.

Today mealtimes have really changed. In many homes both parents are working full-time jobs and home cooked meals are less frequent. Pressure of busy schedules means that there are meals eaten at fast food places or from prepackaged meals. Busy schedules often mean one or more of the family is eating at a different time. Also, TV and phones occupy the attention of people rather than being focused on each other.

Today, mealtimes can be one of the worst times of the day. Everybody wants something different, or they do not like what was made for them. People are coming, going, and choosing to eat at places other than the dinner table together. There are the noises of TV, radio or phones all competing for each other's attention.

I would like to challenge you to do the following three things as it relates to mealtimes.

HAVE ONE MEAL EACH DAY WITH YOUR ENTIRE FAMILY

Why is having a meal together so important? This is the one time each day where everybody is together consistently. It is a time to talk, share about your day and slowdown from the busyness that most people are experiencing. When children are young, they need this time to teach them manners such as sitting still while they eat, asking politely for things they want and thanking the preparer for the food they received. It gives everybody time to slow down and sit together.

Everybody's schedules are different, and our modern world is not as consistent as it was when I was a child, but if you do not make one meal a day a priority it will seldom happen. When our children were growing up, I worked in a job that demanded a lot of hours from me. I made a commitment to Beth and the kids that I would be home for dinner every night. Except for when I had to travel out of town, I missed very few meals over the 20 years our children were home.

For me it meant that I would often get up at 3:30 in the morning to get into work early so that I could leave by 5:00 each day. My boss and co-workers knew this was a priority for me so I seldom had any conflicts that would keep me at work later than that. I looked forward to this time and it built positive experiences for each of us.

BE INTENTIONAL ABOUT PRAYER AND DEVOTIONS

Eating a meal together also gave us the chance to pray together as a family and share a devotional or read the Bible together. We were consistent with the prayer time each day, but our Bible reading, and devotions could have been more consistent. Mealtimes were a time to share, talk and be intentional with the family. It allowed us to talk about what was going on in their worlds and discuss concerns or struggles they may have been facing. One idea for dinner time is to go around the table and have each person share a high and low from the day. This is a way to learn what each person is going through and remember in your prayer time.

Our dinner time had three simple rules that we always tried to follow. First there were no competing interests at the dinner table. The TV was off, no phones and music was off. Second, kids were expected to eat what they were served. We did not make special meals because someone did not like or want something. We did not try to force the kids to eat everything on their plate, but we always were consistent with no dessert or treats unless they ate their dinner. The last rule was that everyone would stay at the table until they were dismissed. They needed to ask for permission to get down to do something else. This was a way to slow them down to eat and eat fast and rush away. These rules helped create normalcy around the dinner table.

MEAL PLANNING

The last thing that we tried to do was allow the kids to be part of meal planning. Letting them get to choose what was being served and to participate in the preparing it. For us, one of the traditions we had was Sunday night pizza. Most Sunday nights we would make homemade pizza for our dinner and since it was a more relaxing time we would often eat while watching a movie or playing games. It made something for the kids to look forward to each week and something a little different from the normal routine.

Figure out a plan that works best for your family. Have a plan. Know what you want to do with mealtimes, be intentional about planning menus and have the kids be part of the planning, preparation and clean up. This is not just mom or dad's role but something that the whole family can be part of.

Reflection Questions:

- How would you describe mealtimes in your family? Crazy, relaxed, stressful?

- What is one thing you want to change to make mealtimes better?

Discussion Questions:

- What is the hardest thing about mealtimes for your family?

- What is one thing you could do to make mealtime a better experience?

- What is your family's favorite meal?

Prayer:

Write a prayer asking God to help you make mealtimes more intentional. Ask Him to help you show your family that mealtimes can be a time of laughter, reflection, and connection.

_____

_____

_____

_____

_____

_____

_____

_____

_____

_____

_____

_____

_____

_____

_____

_____

_____

_____

_____

_____

_____

_____

_____

10 – TECHNOLOGY IMPACTS

Our world has changed dramatically over the past 15 years. The challenges that parents face today are vastly different than the challenges we faced when we were raising our kids. What kids are exposed to and have available to them is far more difficult, challenging, and dangerous today. As a parent, you must be aware of what is going on with technology and have a plan to manage it. Technology by itself is not bad. It has given us help with things that were difficult or time-consuming in the past. But as is true with every good thing there is a dark side that we must watch out for. My experience in this area is limited since my kids were raised before this became so prevalent, but I want to share three guidelines that I believe will help you as parents raising kids in this current time.

SET GUIDELINES

As a parent you are still in control of what your kids have access to. Be responsible and set usage guidelines for technology, whether that is watching TV, playing video games or being on a cell phone. The guidelines should vary by age and school schedule, but you should start by setting clear limits on how long your kids should be using technology. Learning can be done using these technologies, but there are other things that are also important like reading a book, playing with friends, and having quiet time with no technology allowed.

These guidelines should also include content and people with which they can interact. Define what is appropriate and what will be allowed. Do not wait until you have an issue and then try to restrict things. Talk about what they can access and why. I am sure there will be negative reactions and explanations why they should be allowed access to certain things, but remember, you are the parent and set the rules, not them.

MONITOR USAGE

It is not enough to just set guidelines. Your job as a parent is to ensure that the guidelines are being followed. Check in with your children and see what they are watching or what games they are playing. Monitor their phone usage. Know who they are chatting with and about what they are chatting. Let them know that you may ask to see their phone and check what you have been doing at any time. Check into parent monitoring tools like the app KIDSLOX that can restrict access to certain web sites or apps and record what is being done on their phone. Remind your kids that this is not being done to catch them doing something wrong, but to teach them accountability and responsibility.

BE ENGAGED

The best way to be in control of technology is to know what is going on. Know what shows, games and apps kids are watching or talking about. When they want to play a video game, play it with them. You get to see what the game is about and whether it is showing things that you either need to stop or discuss with your kids. When your kids want to watch a show, watch it first and see what it is about. You need to know what your children are watching and if allowed what impact it could have on them. Ask about the apps your kids want to have access to and try them out first. We cannot protect our kids from hearing or seeing things we do not want them to see or hear. But we can teach them how to manage this information and know what to do with it. Setting boundaries and guidelines is a way to help them protect themselves.

As kids become teenagers, having clear boundaries and expectations helps equip kids with tools to fight against peer pressure. When challenged to do something by a peer that is outside their boundaries, having parents to blame gives your kids a way to avoid doing something they know they should not do but still need a reason to give their friends. You are not harming your kids in doing this, you are protecting them and helping them establish boundaries for themselves. When you discover your kids looking at things that are outside the boundaries be careful how you respond. Do not shame them and make them feel guilty for what they have seen, but rather use it as an opportunity to discuss the topic with them and learn about why it is outside of your boundaries. Remember, parenting is about teaching, not punishing.

Watch for the signs that something may be happening. How they respond to your questions will tell you a lot. How they hide or cover up their devices provides hints to what they may be doing. Changes in attitude or behavior may be indications that they are doing something that they know is wrong.

Most issues in technology come from two areas, peer pressure or boredom. Know who your kids' friends are. Invite them to your home and get to know them. Get to know their parents. Understand how their friends are being raised, and if they have different boundaries or morals. Not to judge, but to be aware of the differences in other families and how their boundaries may differ from yours. Keep your children challenged. When they are working on the right things, they will be less likely to be searching for the wrong things. Participate with them in games, reading, puzzles, etc.

And finally, lead your family by example. Look at how you use technology and see if there are any things that you need to change. If you walk around with your face in your phone, it is hard to tell your children to not do the same. Be accountable about what TV shows you are watching and what websites you are going to. If it is not good for your kids to see, the same is true for you!

When we were discussing the use of technology with a friend, he shared this story. He used to always read his Bible using on-line tools like the You Version Bible. These are great resources, but he shared that when he was reading his Bible, all his kids saw was him on the phone. He realized he needed to show his kids and others that he was not playing games on the phone, but that he was actually reading his Bible, so he got out his printed Bible and read from it. Perceptions matter. Use reading your printed Bible to be an example and leave no doubts.

Reflection Questions:

- How well are you monitoring what your kids are watching, listening to, or playing? What do you need to do to improve in this area?

- Have you set limits and expectations with your kids about how they use technology? If not, where do you need to start?

Discussion Questions

- What are your biggest challenges when it comes to technology and your children?

- What has worked for you the most in managing their usage?

- Are there areas of your own technology usage that you need to evaluate and make a change to?

- What are useful Christian sites or apps that you have used for your kids? For yourself?

Prayer:

Write a prayer asking God to help you with technology. Ask Him to help you guide your children in the technological age and that they would be wise and responsible in their use of technology.

_____
_____
_____
_____
_____
_____
_____
_____
_____
_____
_____
_____
_____
_____
_____
_____
_____
_____
_____
_____
_____
_____
_____

11 – MEMORIES THAT CREATE A LEGACY

The last building block is the process of creating memories. We all have memories. Some are happy and some are sad. Events in our life create those memories. As parents, you want to leave your children with as many happy memories as possible. Some experiences are out of our control, such as the death of a parent or family member, but many are within our control.

You need to have building blocks that if you apply them will help you create happy memories in the lives of your children. For us it has been fun to talk with our adult children and ask them about their childhood memories. What things did we do that gave them positive memories and what could we have done better?

The common theme that came across all the memories we discussed involved spending time together. Whether that was with just us as parents or with grandparents or extended family. It was less about what we did and more about spending time together doing things. These memories ranged from going on family vacations, time spent fishing off the dock at the cabin, cabin church and watching mom and dad go on a date together every Saturday night after church. They shared about remembering family dinners together and the fact that mom was home every day after school to welcome them with a snack and a hug as they got off the bus.

Memories do not have to involve spending a lot of money and often the things done at no cost often create the biggest memory. Each person's memories are different. The things that they remember may be different, but by having these shared memories to discuss create special times when we are reminiscing together as a family. Those times when we sit, talk, and laugh together the most.

So how do you create happy memories? I have talked about some of these throughout the book, but I will summarize them here. Build a firm foundation, be intentional and make family members feel special, eliminate unresolved conflict, and allow time for impromptu fun.

BUILD A FIRM FOUNDATION

Having a relationship with Jesus and asking Him to lead your life is where this starts. The right foundation improves your chances of success. This foundation helps you survive the storms in life that all families will go through and help you to maintain and rebuild those happy memories. This is where it all starts. If your faith is not solid, I hope this book will motivate you to ask some questions and seek the answers you need to begin the process of building your life on the foundation of Jesus Christ. This is not about finding a religion or a specific denominational group but rather on forming a relationship with Jesus by asking Him to forgive you of your sins and make him the leader of your life.

This is what you need for yourself and what you desire and pray for your children. **You must teach them that Jesus is our foundation, and everything is built on a relationship with Him.**

BE INTENTIONAL AND MAKE FAMILY MEMBERS FEEL SPECIAL

Creating memories takes work. You must be intentional to create the time and places where those memories can be formed. Being intentional means you are more focused on other people (your children) and what they want than on your own needs and schedule. You create space and times where those memories happen. If you look at your calendar, do you find time written down when you will be focused on doing something with one or all your family? Your calendar is an effective way to see where your priorities are. Too often our spouse or children are the lowest priority on our calendar, and we wonder why they have limited, happy memories. Be intentional to fill your calendar with the time you want to spend together with your family first and then let all the other things fill in around it.

It is okay to say no to things. By saying no to things, it allows your family to know that they are a priority to you. Throughout our life, we always made being present at all the children' activities and school performances a priority. They knew that we would always be there to support them. We also made celebrating birthdays for our children a priority. We created themed birthday events and special activities to show that they were special and worth the investment in time.

Being intentional by creating plans and giving your children something to look forward to is part of the memory making process. But let me give you one caution. Be sure to follow through and live up to your commitments. There is nothing that destroys memories more than unfulfilled promises. When your children are looking forward to doing something with you or with the family and you do not do it, their hearts get broken, and a sad memory is created.

Other ideas to create memories are regular date nights one on one with your children, weekly family game nights, or Sunday night movie nights. I am sure you have your own ideas. As I have said before, it is less about what you do than it is about making it a priority to spend time together.

One other comment on this section. This book is focused on raising children, but I wanted to make a brief comment about your marriage. Your children need to know that your spouse is the most important person after God in your life. Building Godly children comes after you build a Godly marriage. Our children want and need our marriage to be strong. It brings stability and security that all children desire. If you are having marriage issues, make it a priority to do what it takes to get it restored, which may include the next point on unresolved conflict. Children want to see their parents' date. They want to see you having fun. Do not make your children a higher priority than your spouse.

ELIMINATE UNRESOLVED CONFLICT

This is a crucial step in helping to create happy memories with your family. When you have unresolved conflict with your spouse, children, parents, or other family members, you have something that will impact your ability to create happy memories. There will be tension or stress that comes at the worst possible times. This conflict will cause cracks in your foundation that if you do not resolve will grow into bigger problems that will cause the whole relationship to fall apart. Do not put it off because it is hard. Do your part to make sure you have no regrets and wish you had done something. You cannot control how the other person will respond or react or if they will want to move towards restoring the relationship, but you can control what you do to try and restore it. Take what responsibility you need to, seek professional help if you need to, but do not ignore it. Do whatever you need to do to start the process of resolving that conflict you have.

ALLOW TIME FOR IMPROMPTU FUN

Go out and do something fun right now! Do not wait for a plan, just be impromptu and go out and do something. We often have nudges, probably from the Holy Spirit, that we should do something, but we ignore it because it is not in our plan. Sometimes these are the greatest memories. Beth is good about being impromptu. I am much more of a planner. But I have learned over the years that when she says let us do something, I just need to say yes and follow her. Do not try to make sure you have everything figured out first. Do not make sure you are dressed right for the event. Just do it! I missed creating many great memories because Beth or one of the kids suggested something they wanted to do and I said not now, I am busy, or tired or whatever. Those all may have been true, but I missed the moment. Learn to respond with a "yes" when your child says they want to do something with you. They grow up fast and the more times you have said "no," the less they will keep trying and before you know it, they will be grown up and out of the house and those moments will be gone forever. Do not miss out! Put this book down and do something fun right now!

Reflection Questions:

- What are the unresolved conflicts that you have in your life that keep you from creating the happy memories that you want to create?

- What do you need to fix in yourself to address those issues?

- When was the last time you just did something impromptu for the fun of it? Go out and do something right now!

Discussion Questions:

- What are the ways you have tried to create memories for your family?

- How do you make your kids feel like they are a priority in your life?

- What are your favorite family memories?

Prayer:

Write a prayer asking God to help you create lasting memories. Ask Him to help you build a firm foundation, to be intentional about making your children feel special, to resolve conflict and to have fun!

_____

_____

_____

_____

_____

_____

_____

_____

_____

_____

_____

_____

_____

_____

_____

_____

_____

_____

_____

_____

_____

_____

_____

Summary

The purpose of this book was to share with you some building blocks on how you could build Godly children. This is so important because Godly parents who build Godly children create a legacy that can be passed on for many generations. These building blocks are a strong foundation. It is based on a relationship with Jesus Christ and guided by the working of the Holy Spirit. It creates healthy and productive children. We know from history that when someone does not follow this pattern and goes in a different direction it can cause pain and separation.

I am not an expert, but over the course of my life I have learned from the mistakes that I have made and have seen the impact as I watch my children form their families and begin the journey of raising my grandchildren. My hope is that this book will give ideas for you to apply in your family and help you in the process of raising your children.

There is no checklist that says if you do these things your children will become Godly and that you will not have challenges or heart aches. Each person is born as a sinner and must make the choice of following Jesus for themselves. But with the right foundation, and following the building blocks I shared here, you have solid principles that you can apply to help you in the process of raising Godly kids.

Will you make mistakes? Of course, no one is perfect. But as the Bible shows us, we all are given the opportunity to start over and try again. Our children are not looking for perfection. They are looking for honesty, to be loved and cared for, and to know that they are accepted for who they are.

My prayer for each reader of this book is that this book gives you some ideas to help you in the journey of parenthood and points you in the direction of following God and His plans for your life.

One final thought, it is so important to tell our children about God's work in our past and to help them see what He is doing right now. Where has God intervened in your life and made an impact? What is God doing for you now? Your stories and the impact that God has made on your life will form the foundation of your child's belief in God and set their life on the right path.

ABOUT THE AUTHOR

Rick Post is the co-founder and President of Potential Endeavors, a non-profit that helps people to dream, decide and develop. Rick spent 20 years working in a corporate setting and five years of church leadership experience. Potential Endeavors provides coaching, mentoring, development, strategic planning, operational reviews and process improvement for churches and non-profit organizations. We do much of our work in Ukraine as well as with churches in the United States.

Rick lives in Little Canada, Minnesota with his wife Beth and has three adult children, Justin and his wife Maryn, Kala and her husband Sean, and Colin and his wife Katelyn. He also has five grandchildren: Logan, Jack, Luke, Owen, and Chase.

This is Rick's second book. He also wrote <u>Swallowed by a Whale – Twice</u>, which is story of Rick's journey from corporate America to ministry and follows the story of Jonah from the Bible.

If you are interested in learning more about Potential Endeavors, check out our website at potentialendeavors.com.